A Kitten

ERIC ROHMANN

ALFRED A. KNOPF 🐎 NEW YORK

Tale

THIS IS A BORZOI BOOK PUBLISHED BY ALFRED A. KNOPF
Copyright © 2008 by Eric Rohmann
Published in the United States by Alfred A. Knopf, an imprint of Random House Children's Books,
a division of Random House, Inc., New York.
KNOPF, BORZOI BOOKS, and the colophon are registered trademarks of Random House, Inc.
www.randomhouse.com/kids
Educators and librarians, for a variety of teaching tools, visit us at www.randomhouse.com/teachers
Library of Congress Cataloging-in-Publication Data
Rohmann, Eric.
A kitten tale / Eric Rohmann. — 1st ed.
   p.   cm.
SUMMARY: As four kittens who have never seen snow watch the seasons pass, three of them declare the
reasons they will dislike snow when it arrives, while the fourth cannot wait to experience it for himself.
ISBN 978-0-517-70915-3 (trade) — ISBN 978-0-517-70916-0 (lib. bdg.)
[1. Snow—Fiction. 2. Seasons—Fiction. 3. Cats—Fiction. 4. Animals—Infancy—Fiction.] I. Title.
PZ7.R6413Kit 2008
[E]—dc22
2007011093
The images in this book are relief and monotype prints. The artist begins by cutting a key image
(the relief print). Then the color monotype is printed in multiple layers—a layer for each color,
so that each image is the result of thirty to forty separate runs.
PRINTED IN THE UNITED STATES OF AMERICA
January 2008 10 9 8 7 6 5 4 3 2

For my mother and sister,
admired by kittens everywhere.

Once there were four kittens who had never seen snow.

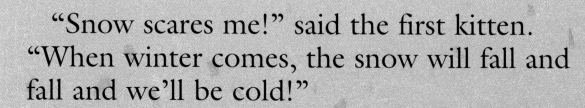

"Snow scares me!" said the first kitten. "When winter comes, the snow will fall and fall and we'll be cold!"

"Freezing cold!" said the second kitten.

"Cold to the tips of our tails!" said the third kitten.

But the fourth kitten said, "I can't wait."

When spring rains gave way to long summer days, the first kitten said, "Today is sunny and warm, but someday snow will fall and fall and we'll be cold and wet!"

"Soaking wet," said the second kitten.

"Wet down to our bones!" said the third kitten.

But the fourth kitten said,
"I can't wait."

When autumn winds ruffled
the trees, the first kitten said,
"Soon the snow will fall and fall.
We'll be cold and wet and snow
will cover everything!"

"Piles and drifts!" said the
second kitten.

"Heaped to our whiskers,"
said the third kitten.

Still the fourth kitten said,
"I can't wait."

Then one winter
morning the kittens
woke to snow.

But the fourth kitten
didn't hide.

He jumped and rolled and laughed.

"Snow! It's cold and wet and covers everything!"

"I can't wait!"